Rhian K. Bhatoe has a love for writing and telling stories. Always trying to find a way that she can get her story to an audience. Even during a time where drama, theatre, and playwriting were not encouraged as a subject. Rhian would write and produce work that has been observed by audiences of all age groups. Rhian has continued to gain experience by attending drama and creative writing groups, working with other organisations and reputable artists. Developing her style as a spoken word artist and writing skills as a poet, she continues to inspire others. Rhian's poetry is poignant to society and can be easily visualised by her readers.

I would like to thank all of my family and friends, past and present. They have given me inspiration to write. To all those that have been a part of this journey. For every experience that we had together and for all the support, opportunities and love that has helped me to keep moving forward.

For my dad, who always had a pen and note pad in his pocket! Thank you for sharing your love of writing poetry with me. This one's for you.

To my angels that protect and guide me towards my destiny. Thanks for always having had faith in me: Parminder 'Trigger' Claire and Winsome J Steele.

Rhian K. Bhatoe

SIMPLY EFFECTIVE

Modern Poetry

AUSTIN MACAULEY PUBLISHERS™

LONDON • CAMBRIDGE • NEW YORK • SHARJAH

A CIP catalogue record for this title is available from the British Library.

ISBN 9781398445291 (Paperback)
ISBN 9781398445307 (ePub e-book)

www.austinmacauley.com

First Published 2022
Austin Macauley Publishers Ltd®
1 Canada Square
Canary Wharf
London
E14 5AA

To my sister, Sharon Bhatoe, and my brother, Prideep Bhatoe, for always believing in my talents. You said I could do it. Thanks.

2 Sides

Once you whispered in my ear,
words I longed to hear.
As you rubbed me down so gently,
we talked all night yet so free.
As we lay under a dim light,
and held each other so tight.

But you told me sweet pretty lies,
That I never saw when lost in your eyes,
It seems you knew how to get your way,
Whilst I didn't see I was being betrayed.
So, as you held me in your arms,
I slowly fell for your charms.

Whilst in a fool's paradise I lay,
You managed to blow me away.
So, as I swam in the sea of love,
You flew away, like a sweet dove.

But I did not notice, that from my river bank you had fled,
So, I continued swimming instead.

Whilst in hope that you would be by my side,
For you, anything you needed I would provide.

But as times gone by, you seem to fade,
and of losing you I am afraid.
As you have accepted my heart, with nothing in return,
What would I have, should you depart?

But yet you fail to realise,
How much you catch me by surprise.
As you continue to avoid what I feel for you,
and continue to take a different view.

Thinking it's acceptable for me to know,
That in the arms of another you can go.
Whilst I dread the thought of being with another,
You feel as though, it's you I smother.

For a love like this is too much for you to take,
So, I guess all along that was my mistake.
To believe that you could love me in return,
But instead, I let our friendship burn.

As you won't hesitate should you get the chance,
to have another lost in your dance.
And as I still spin in your deep whirlpool,
The outside world sees but a fool.
"But this is what will happen and surely can,
If you're his girl, but he's not your man!".

All Alone

I locked off my phone,
Turned down the lights,
Don't want to speak to no one.

Because I got to stop and think!
Because my life's been involved in corruption,
People making their own assumptions,
But this shit, is causing my life disruption.
I can feel the darkness growing inside,
I can feel it drawing from within.

It's going to bring me down, take over my mind,
Make me lose control.
I can hear a voice saying why don't you sell your soul?
I can't think straight, don't know where I'm going.
Which direction should I be taking?
I'm so confused, it doesn't stop spinning.
The walls are closing in and my chest just ceased, 'seriously
I think I can't breathe'!
But I got to get my mind right, get my shit tight,
Dam, I think I can see the light.
There's definitely something at the end of the tunnel.
There's got to be hope for me,

I can do better than this,
Got to work hard for it, going to have to give it my all.
Up in lights they will have my name,
and they will wonder from where I came.
Because love and ambition make the perfect pair,
To get you where you want.

Give yourself drive, set your goals, make sure your heads on straight.
Seriously, think about what you want in life and how you're going to get it.
Don't have regrets to look back on,
Solider it through until your problems are gone.
Make the bad things a learning curve,
Don't let them follow you back around, just let them slip away.
Because when people say 'you can't do it' and you know you can.
It won't take you long to prove.
That all they said it must be wrong,
Because in my heart I'm sure I'm strong.
One day their minds will sway,
Because as beautiful as it is, we all know,
Rome wasn't built in a day!

Birmingham Crew

Hey there, let's not make a scene,
Whether you're from Small Heath, Yardley or Acocks
Green,
Moseley, Selly oak, Bournville and Kings Heath,
All surrounding areas, we don't like causing beef.

So, let me tell you something so you've been warned,
Whether you're from Quinton, Edgbaston or Harborne,
If your heart is in Handsworth, or even Ladywood,
then let's correct those who are misunderstood.

We don't wanna hear chase, sirens and ringing of bells,
so, fix up, if you're living in Perry Barr, Aston, Newtown or
Lozells.

Cause this is what we call the Birmingham crew,
to get through this life, were mistakes are few.
Now, your confidence can allow you,
to keep your head up high,
but that don't mean your people have to die.
Just because you feel,
you've got the wrong things to prove,
instead let's be an inspiration,

to those still in our schools,

Cause it's not over,
no were, not done,
living in this city, we call Brum,

With so many faiths,
Diversity, culture and creed,
we don't run this city, on jealousy and greed.

Shadowed by a reputation,
of shootings, stabbings, gangs, fights, riots,
death and blood shed,
let's get our minds right,
this isn't good for our heads,
instead let's find a way to guide and lead,
for our younger siblings and seeds,
feed your mind with knowledge,
pick up some books,
to give your life a new outlook,
don't need to live by hook or crook,
cause we all need money,
yes, it's true, and when its low,
what can we do,
look in our hearts and stay true,
Override the perceptions, on the news,
looking at life with different views,
to get together and make some real change.
in our hearts and souls,
it doesn't cost a thing.
Finding ways to gain, a little power and respect,

Let's learn how to come correct,
a better way to make bread from crumbs,
let's love our city of Brum,
if your taking drugs to get rid of the pain,
don't distract yourself with budd, pills, glue or crack
cocaine,
change direction, to keep yourself sane,
and to flourish in what you love,
and let it reign,
Cause there's so much hidden talent,
in the city of Brum,
let's show the world,
how it's done,
let them see, how we got it going on,
underground talent,
were we coming from,
Show all those who are misunderstood,
looks like our work, just came out the wood,
but no, it just came out the hood,
whether its music dance, creative arts or fashion,
we're living in a city, with drive and passion,
so, let's get together and make it right,
keep your enemies close, and your homies tight,
so were all here for that little bit longer,
to make Birmingham, that much stronger,
Cause we really are the heart of our country,
let's give it some soul,
creating reputations, we can all uphold.

Cactus Plant and Rain

I wish I was around you more often,
I feel lonely in this place.
Not much around,
To keep me really safe.

I wish I could feel your down pour,
So, I can feel refreshed,
I only need a little and I shall feel blessed.
Without you, my body seems deprived,
So, I always save a little, just to survive.
Because only once in a blue moon,
Do you shower me with your gift?
Whilst I'm surrounded by space,
Where the winds seem to drift.

The seasons are the same, all year round.
And the heat contained, slowly wear's me down.
Unaware of the time, because the days are long,
But me, I'm built to stay strong.

So, I can wait and do without,
Until you relieve me from this drought.
But still, I stand proud and tall,

Until the day you call.

I will breathe again, when I feel you running through my
veins,

As I am your 'cactus plant' and you are my 'rain'.

Crumble and Fall

What will we do, when we crumble and fall?
What will we do, when we crumble and fall?
And the earth shall rise, beneath us all.
For the earth shall continue without man.
After we have destroyed its land.
Taken all that we wish to own,
Ripped apart at the seams of the ozone.
Satellites in the skies, reflecting back on ourselves.
It's not going to happen, no, it's began.
All the damage that's been done.
In the Idle minds of what our future holds,
It's all about money and control.
Cause time is not money, no time is time.
And the days don't pay cash, at the end of the line.
Forgot about the paper trail, our ancestors left behind.
To put forth, what's on our minds.
Express it in music, but what's in store.
'Shake your booty' on the dance floor,
Don't think to quick, the video looks like a triple 'X' flick.
Now sex does sell, but are we all sold out in a world
contrived,
Can't see past the bill board set to entice,
Oh, his chest's out, her skirts thigh high,

I might just go and buy that device.
Take it home and let it take over my life.
Got all the gadgets to stay inside.
And meanwhile our brains are fried.
And outdoors has turned into a dullish grey,
Of poverty death and decay.
While a political speaker, lives in his prime,
Mr, can you explain why so many people have to die?
But no explanations, just alibies,
Cause the mason monster, only has one eye.
Setting his sights on living a lie.
But it's past the point of no return, it's all far gone.
And only God will ensure that justice is done.

The streets shall collapse back into the seas,
The rain forest, may replenish its trees,
The polar, they may refreeze,
And the flowers will be pollinated by the birds and the bees.
But after man is machine and machines are done,
Earth will await the next coming to come.
And they will see that we weren't wise,
And that's why we reached our demise.

Days in Our Lives

I wake up every morning and remember yesterday,
The things I have gotten over, and the things in my way.

I have so many things to do,
with so many done.
Looking at things I have past,
and things yet to come.

But what will come from your day,
never do you know.
What you shall learn
and what you shall show.

I wonder if the sun will shine,
and I shall find a glow.
Or if my day will be grey and bleak,
with time so very slow.

But if I enter into my day,
with the right frame of mind.
Things come so much easier,
and my paths easier to find.
So, I lift my head high and do what I feel is right.

So, the less in life, do I have to fight.

So today I won't worry, about my tears and sorrow.
Because then again, there's always tomorrow.

Demons and Angels

I look towards my left shoulder, then I look towards my
right,
To one side such beauty and on the other quite a fright.
For upon my left sits an angel with wings,
With a perfect halo, innocence it brings.
To keep me feeling positive, it shall all be ok,
With the power she brings she shall get me through the day.

Then with just a swift turn and darkness is in sight,
The Demon that can extinguish the light.
For when I am in darkness, depression and despair,
It seems that only my demons are there.
'Care for no one, as on one cares for you',
They shall not understand your honesty, so there's no need
to be true.

And now he calls you a thief in the night for you have stolen
his heart,
But with the roles in reverse, you had to play the part.
But angel says 'I loved with all my body, passion heart and
soul.'
But the demon seems to have control.
For my love has become hurt and pain

And sanity has become insane.
The voices in my head are ringing loud and sharp,
I require a melody, a symphony of harps.
As the demons say 'why not just think about yourself?'
In a society where no one wants to help.
But angel say 'just keep on going, with such positive energy and flow,
Take wisdom from others, it will help you to grow.
Take the energy that surrounds you and the spirit within,
Don't let the demon trap you, inside your sins.
Because when you fall for gluttony, greed and lust,
Look to your angels for contentment, honesty and trust.

Every Time

Every time I hold you and look in your eyes,
I see the man I love and realise,
That for you, anything I will do,
as long as you hold me, in your arms too.

I will sleep by your side,
if you will hold me tight,
I will tell you my wrongs,
if you can help me, put them right.

I will tell you my secrets every time,
if you promise not to tell.
for my feelings that go deeper,
then if I had a wishing well.

Every time I say your name,
my knees get weak,
My hands perspire and I get cold feet.
Every time you walk in the room, my blood starts to bubble.
My temperature's so high,
with you there's never a reason to be shy.

Every time I just think of you,
I feel you round my back,
Every time I smell the scent of you,
my mind goes off track.
So, I would like to say "thank you", just for being mine,
and for being there for me, when I call *every time.*

Fools of Love

You made everything seem nice and cool.
So, I guess when it comes down to it, I'm just a fool.

I thought everything was so perfect,
I thought everything was so right,
cause you were the one I thought of every day and night.

You said you loved me and I was the one,
but I turned my back for a second and you were gone.

You said you'd be here forever,
but forever didn't last.
So, I guess I have to look to the future,
because now you're in my past.
But still I can't understand where it all went wrong,
so here it comes again, I've got another sad song.
So, you didn't realise what you had,
but you will while I'm gone.
And to get over you, that won't take me to long.

As never did I think that from you would come something so
cruel.
But you can only be a fool of love, if you only love a *fool*.

Friend in You

Have you ever felt confused about where to go?
Or which direction is life taking?

When all seems to be going wrong and your dreams are
breaking,
Your spirits are low and you've lost all hope,
Everything's too much and you just can't cope.
Can life be what we make it.

Look in your heart and find the strength,
To wake up and shake it.
Put determination into what you love and try to live your life
completely,
Put your thoughts into action, rather than thinking too
deeply.
Because when you pause and your life's on hold,
No money in your pocket and your future seems cold.
Need the kind of money we can fold.

Put your mind to it because it's never too late.
Take control of your life and your own fate.
Take it step by step, task by task and round by round,
Don't let anyone try to bring you down.

Learn from the bad and thrive from the good,
Make sure all your actions are understood.
Know those who are close and try to ignore your foes,
Believe in yourself, until it shows.
Because when you are your best friend,
You will be together until the very end.

Friends Choice

I choose my friends wisely.
I choose my friends with care.

I choose the kind of friends who will always be there.
The ones who will crake a joke, "when I need to smile",
And tell me "every thing's ok" once in a while.

The kind of friends you can share all your secrets with.
And the ones who never say "I told you so", even though
they did.

So, I guess I choose my friends wisely,
Because wise they should be.
But most of all I choose my friends,
to be just like me.

From One Moment
to the Next

How do things change in the blink of an eye?
How does something change, when you haven't realised?

one moment I'm in love with you,
and the next I don't feel the same.
one moment I want to hold you close,
then I fear you're playing games.

Do things only change,
when I'm not really sure,
or if things just aren't the same,
as they were before.

if it's for the moment, then I guess it's just for then,
but do you know if you're having a moment, or even when.

if someone does something for the moment,
then what could they do.
hurt, cheat, kill or steal.
Or say "I love you".

sometimes it's nice to have a moment all to yourself,
and sometimes it's best to share your moment with someone
else.
But never shall you know,
What will happen for the best?
As you will never know what will happen,
From one moment to the next.

God's Religion

Oh, dear God.
How can I call upon thee?
In a world with such controversy,
Over religion, your rules and regulations.
If there's only one of you,
Then why, so much complications?
So many differences of opinion,
Wars of belief and contradictions.

Is religion a map, which has many roads?
Taken from where our seeds are sowed,
Different paths to follow and direction to take,
For us all to end up, in the same place.

To reach the one true almighty,
The one who created us all,
And all the powers that be,
The winds that blow and the force of our seas.

The mind of mankind and the cycle of life,
From beginning to end and the afterlife.
Do you control the gates to Nirvana or Heaven?
And will the path I choose, take me to cloud eleven.

Or shall I be held high or low, in your esteem,
If my path should take its own regime.
Oh God, would you give me the strength to carry on,
If I followed the teachings of the Koran,
Or would you still help me through grief,
If I followed the scripts of the Guru Granth Sahib.
Or do I need to bear a cross and learn from the Holy Bible,
Just to make my existence viable.

Would it matter at all, if I called for you?
As Allah, Guru, Messiah or Christ,
Or would the sound of my cries suffice.

Would I need to speak to you from a,
Synagogue, mosque, temple or church?
Just so that my prayers are not left in the lurch.

Because I'm sure that if you are Hindu, Sikh, Christian
Or Shinto like the Japanese,
You still hold the power, to bring us to our knees.
If your Jewish, Buddhist or Muslim,
You still provide us with hope,
When this world is looking grim.

Did you create religion for the purpose?
Of personal choice, diversity and belief?
Or are we forced to go to war,
To feel sorrow death and grief?
Would a turban suffice, a veil or the robes of the pope?
For you to full fill me with happiness and hope.

Does my skin need to be, as rich as chocolate?
As pure as milk or with a hint of honey?
And would my poor soul still be worthy,
If I wasn't rich with money?

Could I still control my karma?
And would you still write my fate?
Regardless of my religion, if I promise to emulate.

For I see, that you see over,
The beauty in this one world, you have built.
And all those that have reached you,
After their blood has been spilt.

But can you help us to realise,
That those who fail to compromise,
Shall one day bring us all to our demise!

Green Eye

He says I'm the sweetest thing he ever met,
Someone he will never forget.
The way he picks up on my sex appeal.
Hey girl 'I know you're a steal'
He says the way I love him, its off the hook,
Smart, clean and can cook.
He loves the way I'm head strong.
Can stand up for myself.
A powerful woman, doing it for herself.
He says he likes that I have ambition,
He knows I'm going to go far.
He knows I strive for the stars.

So, I am who I am and I be who I be,
Straight up, will he love me for me.
So, I push for my career and work really hard,
Still taking his feelings into regard.
Trying to run my house and home,
Do a performance, write a poem.
So, I don't ask him for his money, I don't ask for much help,
For him I just wish happiness and health.
For him to know he has a woman right by his side,
In unison when our worlds collide.

But his green-eyed monster seems to have taken hold,
Oh, wait I think it's got full control.
And now my strong mindedness, is just me being stubborn.
And my sex appeal, just make men glutton.
And my outgoingness is all a bit much,
I really should know when to shut up.
And now to have my own opinion,
Just means 'ah, she can't be told.
And that understanding we had, the winds blow cold.
Am I too hot to handle, too hot to hold,
I should really call the ghost busters, because he's out of control.

He can't put out my inner flame, that is my eternal glow,
So, with resentment and despair, I had to refrain from his chain,
To show him that I cannot be contained.
So, it finally became apparent, without hesitation or delay,
That two hopeful hearts are now left astray,
Hoping to find love, for their own unique ways.

Happiness

Happiness is something which you can achieve,
If you do not allow your heart and soul to be deceived.
Be true to the one within and those who care,
And your happiness shall be worthy to share.
To achieve all you want in life, find a way of taking things
as they come.
Don't let things get you down, look up, when your feeling
glum.
Look to your spiritual self to provide you with love and
wealth,
To grow your mind and good health.

Do your best to enjoy the special things in life,
And be wise to all the negative people and strife.
Take each moment slowly as you continue upon your
journey of tests,
Walking a path of challenges? Then put a little pep in your
step.
Use the knowledge and wisdom you hold,
To put a smile on your face and take control.
Squeeze out the wet blankets and leave them out to dry,
Take all the 'haters' and 'teeth graters' and put them to one
side,

And though life can be tough sometimes,
I know the grass is always greener when I have tried.

How Prominent Am I?

Amongst those who surround me I shine bright as a star,
I know their live would be different without me,
I'm sure of that by far.
With my caring nature, originality and soul,
With such a character, spirit and flow.
But when God descended me to this earth,
Was he sure I could make a difference?

To my parents I'm youngest of five,
A surprise child that was set to thrive.
Set to follow my path,
Though I do take traits from mum and dad,
Hoping to make them proud and make them glad.
And to my brothers and sisters its quite prominently true,
That if I was never born, they might take different views.
I know that they would be different for sure,
But for them, what would have been in store.

My friends, I choose them wisely and they choose me right
back,
Because they see it so clearly, prominently a fact.
They say, you have such grand qualities, those that a mate
should make,

Strong friendship bonds that don't easily break.
Through thick and thin and for goodness' sake,
Side by side, through ups and downs,
Friendships that are prominently found.

So, I know I have a purpose, I know there's a reason for me,
Someone who stands out, quite prominently.
For I bring with me beauty with a burning flame inside.
The kind of passion no one can override.
So, I shall stand proud, stand tall and if times I do fall,
Then I shall pat away the dust and do as I must.
So those who still yet fail to see,
Shall notice me quite prominently.

In Limbo

My heart longs for you, because I miss your touch,
I want you right here because I miss you so much.

But when I try to hold you close, I feel as though you push
me away,
When I ask you if I should leave, you say 'you want me to
stay'
The arguments seem to be worth their weight in gold,
And the way we used to feel, now seems old.

Because when love starts to deteriorate,
It can leave you in a mess and such a state.
In limbo with your love, but at what cost.
Would we be better without each other or would we feel
lost?
It seems we are comfortable with our silences or do we have
nothing to say.
As we try to please each other, but still have it our own way.

How can we believe its love, when were not really sure?
Is it each other we want or are we looking for more?
The kind of relationship where questions are not so far away.
About how we feel and if we should stay?

For all the memories we have shared, now we live our lives apart,
Trying to hold on from a distance, how can we share our hearts.

Because deep down I really do wish, that our love held the power,
But this feeling in my stomach, tells me it's going sour.
Is there any coming back from this or will our love just fade?
Is our relationship what we make it or is it what we've made.

Interracial Relationship

The way we walk together makes us want to smile,
The way we dress we got culture and style.
My face is looking so cute,
Your bodies looking like forbidden fruit.
We treat each other like a king and queen,
But people are starting to make a scene.

Saying 'why don't you just stick to your own'
Because of the difference in our complexion and tone.
But in our kingdom, we sit proud on our thrones,
While society let's use know we have to go at it alone.
Because people show it in their faces when they frown,
Think its ok to make us the talk of the town.

We do come from a different way of life,
But that didn't stop us from becoming man and wife.
Regardless of the colour of our skin,
We'd both bleed red, if we lost a limb.

Was it meant to be, could we call it fate,
Two different tastes eating off the same plate.
Do they really have the right to be-little?
two different roads that have met in the middle.

For them to judge the thoughts of two minds,
And all that their hearts find.
They say 'it will never work, it's no good',
Can people really be so misunderstood?
About all that love can hold, as the colour of your skin,
Won't keep you warm in the freezing cold.
Because feelings and emotions don't come in shades,
You make me feel like I'm a high grade.
The way we touch, we got it going on,
Does it really matter where we are from?
Our minds meet on another level,
Where in each other's interests we revel.
Learning more than what we know,
Think we've been hit by cupid's crossbow.

Now we are friends, lovers and so much more.
Could our loving be this hardcore?
Wake up those living in the dark ages like dinosaurs,
Because there are no fossils in our relationship,
We have been explored.

Intro into Author History

A premature push … push as I entered the world,
Congratulations it's a beautiful baby girl.
1980 on the 6th May,
Was a child born, to lead her own path way.
My mother called it stubborn,
Maybe it's the Taurus in me, but why the delay,
The choice of letting time pass by has a price to pay.
I was a bright spark in class, always willing to read out loud
and proud.
The teachers said I was a joy to teach.
Pleasant, popular, enthusiastic and not afraid to speak.

I wasn't afraid to make friends of all varieties and kinds,
Brown, black, white or other, please specify!
The best way to see people, was not to judge, except on what
they done.

Started secondary school with bigger people,
I was a little scared, but taught to be confident and prepared.
Knowing a few people in the school, I made friends easy.
And having elder brothers and sisters in the same school,
made it breezy.
Tried to keep my head in my books,

To learn about life and to give myself new outlooks.
For my dad always told me 'it's not who, but what you know'
Don't follow people like a domino.
Use your own instincts to reach your limits.
Don't be lonely, but sometimes stand alone.
And my mother taught me,
about what a woman should and should not condone.
Stand up straight, proud and tall.
Hold your head up when you walk in the street,
You have no reason to be looking at your feet.
Make sure your nose is not too high,
Or you may miss opportunities that pass you by.

So, I did do my studies but we can all go off track,
As a teenager, life goes like that.
Missed a few lessons chilling with my crew,
Thought all of it was so cool.
But to be honest much of it never did me any good,
Had to catch up quick, if a chance of passing still stood.

But you have to grow up quick in this day and age,
Responsibilities come fast with a constant flow,
They can get you giddy like you have vertigo.
I can feel the impact blow by blow.
Is someone aiming their crossbow.
As I grow older wisdom starts to play its part,
Oh, 'this is what they must have meant at the start'.

I have been through some lessons in life as all is never as it
seems,
In reality, people do have shattered dreams,
We have sorrow, heart ache, disbelief and distrust,
But as much as it pains us, we learn to adjust.
Learning to share loving moments with the people I care for
most,
Family and friends that should be treasured,
In the spirit of good hope.

As life goes by, the possibilities still seem endless.
I realised the office job was not for me,
It is time to let my true love free,
The love from within, the freedom of speech, expression and
poetry.
Though I know life can be hard, I know we have to face it,
And to reach our dreams and goals, well I know we have to
chase it.
Because in our own lives, when we decide to take control,
Who knows what the future hold?

Isolator

Isolator, isolator, I am an isolator.

Stay in your homes, you've been told,
It's for your own safety,
There's a deadly virus, gone out of control.
It takes your last breath and sucks out your soul,
It's a biological weapon, don't need no guns.
It's not a holiday, it's no fun.
It's not pretend, this isn't a show,
Its killing people like dominos.
Across the world, across the seas
It's not blowing over, it's not a tease.
So please do take it seriously.

Isolator, isolator, I am an isolator.

Do it for other's and save lives,
Keep your distance, or don't be surprised,
Reduce the risk to those, who are trying to help.
Keep yourself, too yourself.
Corona virus or Covid 19,
Wash your hands and keep things clean.
Be mindful of others, families, neighbours and friends

Those that maybe at a loose end.
Look out for those that are elderly or that have ill health,
Where in this together, no matter of status and wealth.

Isolator, isolator, I am an isolator.

Don't be greedy and learn to share,
A simple gesture to show you care,
Check on people down the street,
But make sure, your distance is more than 2 feet.
You may have symptoms or maybe none at all,
But it seems, this invisible virus can crawl.
From one person or object to the next.
A simple droplet or a breath.
It doesn't have feelings, it doesn't hate,
It's not racist and it doesn't discriminate.

Isolator, isolator, I am an isolator.

Try not to fear, but have some sense,
Don't visit your family and friends.
And if you can't be with your man or girl tonight,
then send them a message or a skype.
Give them a call, check their ok.
But don't go around to stay.
Keep loved ones at home and try to live good,
Life can be tough when you live in the hood.
But keep upbeat, stay positive and strong!
Hopefully we will beat this, in not too long.
Big thanks to NHS and volunteering crew,
Together, we can get through,

So, whatever we do, at least we tried.
I hope to see you on the other side.

Isolator, isolator, I am an isolator.

Just A Quick Coffee

Good afternoon sir, please take a seat,
Would you like a little something to eat?

Oh no dear, I feel quite beat.
Just need to take a load off my feet.
I think I'll just have a drink, if I may miss,
What do you recommend?

Well, there's this,
We have a cappuccino, mocha, latte, espresso double or
small,
'A latte, in a glass that's tall'
A latte sir, that's just Italian for milk.
Would you like that hot or cold?
Hot with an espresso!
Ok sir, that's one café latte sold.

So, as he awaits his warm coffee cup,
His mind gently drifts away,
As to where his coffee may come from,
And exactly how it's made.
For coffee beans were not found it seems,
Until the ninth century in Ethiopia.

In lands of high.
But now we have filtered, instant and dry,
In high supply,
All across the world.

As his drink arrives, he replies,
Is it ok to smoke?
As I do like a cigarette with my coffee.
Oui Monsieur, how very French.
En Chante, Sil vous plait.
For you Sir, one café au lait.

Now alone with his drink,
He has a moment to think,
and clear his mind from all his worries.
As he cups his hands around his glass,
His palms are warmed from a freeze.
As the aroma of his coffee fills the air, in a gentle breeze.
So, he takes a sip with a frothy lip, of milk steamed to perfection.
Just right he thinks, thanks to 'Lino Meiorins' creation.
For his customers thought his Italian cappuccinos were a bit too strong,
So, he made them long, with extra milk and called them café lattes.

So, as his drink came to an end.
He said thank you and see you again,
And was happy to have just stopped for a quick coffee!

Last Word

It may be too late as I write down these words,
Because I delayed, in saying all I had to say.
Now the sky has clouded over and I see nothing but grey.
I wish I could see your face, but fate doesn't sway,
For I am out of time as you have descended to the other side.
You were like a brother, bonified.
But we allowed distance between us holding onto ego and
pride.
I never got to tell you how I loved you so,
A friendship so priceless it could not be bought with jewels
or gold.
Now I inscribe my message in to this scroll,
Hoping it will reach your soul.
When you watch me from up above, being the Angel, you
are,
Whilst I hold onto memories in my heart.
Of the times we laughed and cried,
Personalities that had been identified,
With honesty and respect that had been clarified.

Over time jokes were shared and a few harsh words too,
But always with the best of intentions, through and through.
I had funny one liner and you loved your gadgets,

Splitting our sides, working in the garden chopping weeds
with hatchets.
I thought you would be here forever, I would never of had a
clue,
That for the rest of my life, you would be gone out of the
blue.
I wish I had said more often, just how special you are,
But caught up in the chaos of life, those moments were not
shared,
Although in the depths of our hearts we both know we cared.
I still feel your presence guiding me in the right direction,
Although life is full of question.
You still give me a sign, when my stars are aligned,
while my intuition gives me peace of mind.
And though it may seem absurd, I know that you hear.
My last words.

Life After Death

A shudder of disbelief,
As this feeling seems to creep,
Upon me slowly,
It's not quite sinking in.
What was it, that you just told me?
Feeling suffocated,
How can I breathe?
Knowing you just took your last breath.
Is my life over?
Now, that you've been taken by death.

Where shall you go,
A free spirit, with soul.
But your absence is apparent,
In my self-contained world.
Where nothing shall ever be the same,
Where do I place this pain?
That cuts from the inside out,
Following a long, lonely road of doubt.
As my heart screams aloud, for help.
My silent cries fall upon deaf ears.

Can no one hear the shattering?
Of broken hearts and dreams.
But from the rays of the sun,
I feel you beam.
As if you were still by my side,
And our future hadn't died.

Another life, taken so sudden.
Another life taken in a flash,
Minds lost in vengeance and wrath.
Taking you to a place unknown,
Where you shall roam,
And watch me from near,
In a space where, your time has not yet come,
But now, there's nothing to fear.

Or were you reborn,
Into the face of another,
A new child to a father and mother,
Given a chance to start a fresh,
Or to re-live, all life's tests.

A spirit reincarnated into another recognizable form,
To touch new hearts and keep them warm.
Or does my faith believe,
That your existence so pure,
Yes, I'm sure.
That God has welcomed you with open doors.
As I sense your eyes,
Watching me through the skies,
And with such power,

No evil can touch me so.
Cause, my angels spread their wings,
And bring me such things,
That cannot be found upon this earth.
To trust the instinct within,
That believes in myself worth.

To all my friends lost young.
Those taken before their time,
Those who were taken by corruption and crime,
Those that were innocent,
But in the wrong place at the wrong time.
I receive you and see the signs.
From where you may have reached the gates,
To an existence divine.
Providing me,
Not with standard visions or De ja vu,
But messages inside my dreams of truth.
Whilst we continue to survive,
Upon hell itself.
Weighing out love and wealth.
Lost in some head spinning confusion.
Cause is a life worth less than power,
Is a life worth less than pride?
Is a life worth less, than the compassion you find inside?
If a life can be taken so sudden,
Then where do I stand.
Well, I guess my life is unknown,
And death, well that's just out of my hands.

Live and Forgive

How do we know if we shall see each other tomorrow?
Or what lays around the corner.
The things we take for granted and the things we let be,
For what will happen in the future, we shall not see.

For if today I can't tell you 'I'm sorry' and you're not here
when I am,
Then I ask you to forgive me now, right here when you can.

Did I ever tell you that I love you so, because in my heart I
really do?
And if we're not here tomorrow, I'll know how much you
knew.
Because sometimes we might take for granted, the things we
have now,
Relationships, family and friends, to show your feelings
how.
To take a situation, just as I see as my pride may let things
be,
But to have the strength and energy to take a chance,
On allowing our lives to live their dance.

For if we're not here tomorrow, I'd at least like you to know,
That I was not afraid to let my feelings show.
So, learn to let live and to really forgive, if you really care,
Because tomorrow the people you love,
They just might not be there.

Love Struck

My love for you seems to overpower my soul,
It makes me do things I'm not happy with.
We used to be so good together, all the things we shared and
did.
But now it's all changed, we have gone our separate ways.

I have to go at it alone.

My mind is full of thoughts that seem to make me crazy,
The days are passing by but everything is hazy.
All the arguments and fights that seem to take place,
Over all that never really mattered, case by case.
I wonder why my heart fights me when my mind wants to be
free.
A constant daily battle, with me, myself and I,
Wanting to get over you, who would have thought I'd have
to try.
Sitting here convincing myself that it's all for the best,
I just thought it would have ended, the day that you left.
But you're on my mind, every moment I get to think.
It seems I was mistaken about the whole situation,
There were times of happiness as well as frustration.
So, I can keep myself busy, well at least day by day,

Trying not to let thoughts of you pass my way.
Walking around all starry eyed,
But hollow inside.
Now between love and loss, I am stuck,
I ask myself, why oh why?
Then a voice replied,
"I think you're love struck!"

Me and My Myalgia

We wake up every morning.
With the rise of day.
I want to get out my bed,
But Myalgia is in my way,
I now know him as Algia,
For that's he's new name,
Some of you may recognise him,
or know him as pain.

Wake up Myalgia, wake up.
But Myalgia feels slow,
Because he's heads ringing,
And every part is tingling,
From head to toe.
So, In a drowsy daze,
I rub my eyes,
As he's back ache co-insides.
We shake a leg,
Get out of bed,
And thank the lord that I'm not dead.

Ready for a day that's new,
Full of opportunities in my head.

But Myalgia has other ideas instead.
He wants to play up,
and he takes up my time,
He wants attention.
But doesn't want to wait in line.
He springs up when I least expect him so,
then holds on tight and doesn't let go.

When I go to work,
He has to come with me!
Maybe it's a good job, that he can't be seen.
Because he really is invisible to others,
They can't see him by my side.
They really do think it's all in my mind.
"Hey, it's probably, in your head"
I should call "algia", "Right," said Fred.
My imaginary friend, always on my back,
He distracts me and stops me in my tracks.
He slows me down, with a voice in my ear,
Oh, be careful, don't overdo it dear!

So, I try to relax, for the evening,
But he can't keep still,
Should he sit or stand, stand or sit,
Jump up and exercise, just a little bit,
Relax, meditate, do tai chi,
Or by 6:30 he could just go to sleep.
He's not full of much adventure.
Sometimes he feels a bit down in the dumps,
Others don't understand and still expect him to jump.
He's anxiety can get high and his nerves all over the place,

A shaky situation, hard to bring it back to base.
A little too much tension, not enough mention.
So, as he takes time to wind down for the night,
I wrap him up in a blanket,
So, he's all snug and tight.
Hopefully today we can get some rest
And tomorrow, well put our friendship to the test,
Let's hope we can do our best.

More Money

More money, more money,
Is it the dream your chasing, or is it the fame and ratings?
For all the finer things in life,
Think it will relieve us from struggle and strife.
Can we all live in harmony while where on the grind.
More money, more money we are working overtime!

It's all about the money debts and fees,
People's heads getting blown because of G's.
Because you can make it, spend it, break it or fake it,
But let me tell you, it doesn't grow on trees.

Because monies what make this world go around,
A Doller a Dime or a Pound.
Getting educated to work and get paid.
Then sitting down and calculating how much you made.
You need money, if you wanna wear Versace, Parada or
Donna Karen New York.
Even if you want to eat your dinner with a fork.
Because the best things in life are not free,
For everything in life, you pay a price or a fee.

Because more money, more money, and the 'happier I'll be'
If I was rolling, would I be feeling ecstatically?
Living life to the max, wouldn't you want to join me,
more money, more money, oh yes indeed!
But don't let it possess you, keep your spirit free.
Because monies like poison, it's deadly.

Whether you're a grabber, a lender a spider or a spinner,
it starts with money, but it can make you a sinner.
As people have their own interest and it's going to rise,
Do so much for it, truth or lies.
It may buy you what you desire or does it enforce greed,
Is it something you chase or do you take lead?
You can live for money, kill for money, but it won't help,
If what you do, is just for yourself.
You can see it pass for day to day,
You can save it, spend it or give it away.

Because more money, more money, and the 'happier I'll be'
If I was rolling, would I be feeling ecstatically?
Living life to the max, wouldn't you want to join me,
more money, more money, oh yes indeed!
But don't let it possess you, keep your spirit free.
Because monies like poison, it's deadly.

Morning Rush

As I get ready, to leave my house,
On this cold and frosty morning,
People are in the streets,
whilst the days just dawning.

So, I'm wrapped up in layers of clothes,
just to keep warm,
cause later they said,
"There's going to be a storm",
But first I must concentrate, on getting to work,
Cause if I'm late, my boss will go bezerk,
He's not really a friendly chap,
Always stressed out, about this and that,
But I really do, need to make it on time,
Oh, here's my bus,
Oh dear, that's not mine.

Public transport, it really is a joke,
"I agree", the man next to me spoke.

All the children are off to school,
Adults in traffic, trying to keep their cool.

oh, here's my bus, oh wait,
it didn't stop,
went straight passed,
not even to, drop.
I don't believe this,
how long will I have to wait?
better call work,
tell them, I'm running late.

Oh well, here we go,
the buses have come, two in a row,
So, as I get on the bus,
well, there's no seat,
so, I guess I'll have to stand,
upon my feet,
As the driver, is now trying to be quick,
All the jerking of this bus,
is making me sick.

Oh well, there seems to be a seat free,
I think I'll take, that one for me.

People reading papers, and listening to some IPad3,
Holding conversations and having to squeeze.

So, I rang the bell, as it approached my stop,
got off and had to pop in the shop,
ran to work all the way through town,
trying to get through the rain,

as it came down,
got into work, and brushed down the dust,
Oh, I do hate the morning rush.

My Mother's Day

Hi mum, I bought you some flowers,
And a box of chocolates too,
For the scent you have and your sweetness too.

A mother's love that is so dear,
At times of despair and fear.

For I feel you guide me,
To watch wrong from right.
Showed me to thank God and pray at night.

My mother's strength,
It shines from within.
As bright as the sun,
Like when my days begin.

Her support is always by my side,
Even when she has to bring me down to size.
To understand that it's all for the best,
Helping me to get through all life's tests.

A mother's love,
That was suckled on from birth,

How could I ever doubt, my mother's worth?
When she's the woman, who I will probably turn into,
Well, that's just fine with me mum, if I'm just like you!

Re-Born

You tell me you love me, like it's a God sent,
Tell me what I want to hear, but your body shows me
different.
Cause when I ask you for the truth, only lies do you tell.
So, it's time for me to say, "farewell".
For my love was true and pure,
And all that came with you I was willing to endure.
Dramas, when they get you down,
I'd be the girl to turn around your frown.

When you come home from a hard day's work,
I'd cook some food, help you relax, with everything on
point,
It is a shame that you had to disappoint.
Cause even though you had all this love at home,
You had to go elsewhere,
tell me how I'm supposed to believe,
For me you always there.

When for those moments you can forget about me.
Whilst my tears cry the deepest sea.
So, no more tears to drown my sorrow,
Should have left you yesterday, can't leave it for tomorrow.

For all the love I had, I would take all the strife,
But your sharp lies, cut me like a knife.
Now do I sit here and let my heart bleed,
or accept the fact, that I have been deceived.

From someone who I wanted, as my all,
instead, you pushed me, for a long fall.
And now that I've fallen flat on my face,
With my pride, that has been disgraced.
Cause you thought you were a player,
I guess you've been played out,
Say you want me back, but I don't want a "boy scout".
Cause I'd rather be alone, then be the fool,
Your choice, has been overruled.

Wanted to have girls in the street, and a wifey at home,
Didn't you see what I was worth, "there is no clone."
Thought it would be acceptable to play me,
Sorry babes, you got more chance on "the PS3".
So, it's time for my life to take a different direction,
need a man with less imperfection.

Thought our love was magic, like a unicorn,
But either way, my hearts been torn,
So I'll forget about this dead relationship and be reborn.

Sack-Man

What do you do when you're in love?
and you don't know if he loves you back,
Or, how do you know, if you really love him,
Or if he's just good in the sack.
Don't get it confused if it's just sex,
no matter if you feel he's the best.

Does he buy you a dozen roses to brighten up your day?
Will he sometimes compromise so you get your own way?
Does he sing you a love song that comes, straight from the
heart?
Or, is it not the same, as it was at the start?
Does he look at you, like you're the most precious thing in
the world.
And would he for no reason at all, buy you diamonds and
pearls.

Does he tell you all his problems, so that they can be shared?
And when did he last show you, how much he cared.
Does he hold you tight, in bed at night, as if he wants you
close?
Or do you not feel him until, your morning tea and toast.

You may get butterflies, when you see him from across the
room.
But does he get weak at the knees, at the scent of your
perfume.
Does he miss you after just one day or two?
Or is he happy to see you once a week, and that will have to
do.

Does he show you that he thought of you?
when you weren't even there,
Or, does he come home and prove, that he has been
elsewhere.
You may trust in every word he says,
But is he telling you the truth,
Or does he hold back on his words,
as he grits on his tooth.

Does he know how to surprise you,
When you least expect it so,
Or do surprises, seem so long ago.
Will he massage your body after a hard day's work?
Or will he shrug his shoulders, say "No", then give you a
smirk.

Does he know to give you a kiss and a hug, when you need it
most,
Or, does he seem, like a guest, to whom you are a host.
Does he show you; you can trust him?
because he never shows you, you can't,
or do you take in his lies, as if they enchant.
Leaving you unsure, of how you really feel,

and why you love him so?
or without holding on, you should let him go.
Because to love and lose,
maybe better, then not being loved back.
So just make sure your man is worth more,
Then what he does in the sack.

Thank You, Lord

I'd like to say to someone, who I can rely upon,
Someone who is never gone,
When I need to know, I just Pray,
Then you send a message in your own way.

Whenever in trouble, I say Grace,
Cause you have put a miracle in every face.
In millions of people you have put hope,
And have made me feel I can cope.
For somethings you make me wait,
And for others, well I just call it fate.

Now, dear lord, i thank thee for life,
For carrying me through strife.
For watching me from above,
And for sending me much love.
But, oh god, if in days of pleasure i forget thee,
Then I only ask one thing, please remember me.

So, now's my chance to thank the lord,
for all I ate and every glass poured,
for bringing the sun after rain,
And for bringing relief after pain,

For helping me get through sorrow,
and for looking forward to tomorrow,
For giving me family and friends,
the things we treasure until the end.

Now dear lord, i thank thee for life,
For carrying me through strife,
For watching me from up above,
And for sending me much love,
But, oh god, if in days of pleasure i forget thee,
Then I only ask one thing, please remember me.

Thanks Sis

At times I may forget how valuable sisters are,
Sometimes I may feel, that you're a bit too far.
But I'm glad to know that you are there,
When I need a friend, sister you always care,
You don't judge what my problem is,
You still help and try to be fair.
So, I'd like to take this chance to say,
"Thank you, for being you!"
Because now I can't imagine my life,
Without my sisters, what would I do?
Always there when I need to talk and have a little moan,
Even when I call you, all het up and talking out of tone.
But I hope you know, that as your sis, I'm here for you too.
If you want to talk after a hard day,
We could take a different view,
To chill out, laugh and relax, I will be right on que.
So do not worry sister, for you have a sister that loves you
so,
Together seeds from the same pot,
that continues to blossom and grow.

The Crossover

Did you say 'it was like, we were meant to meet for a
reason'?
Well I agree and it is quite pleasing.
To have planted a friendship seed,
That has blossomed indeed.
Into both our hearts and souls,
How it happened, is a story to be told.

Whilst I'm in your presence,
I get this tingly feeling inside,
Like as if you're a present,
All wrapped up in a bow, just for me.
I know we both feel the chemistry.

Like when we can't stand, eye contact for too long,
Because this feeling might be too strong.
Holding back and questioning "would this be right or
wrong?"
But we both know each other and we both like what we
know,
You fill me with sunshine and I bring out your inner glow.

As we provide each other with comfort, to speak open
honest and free,
Whilst we catch some jokes and act stupidly.
And when I needed rescuing, you were my shining knight,
And in my darkest hour, I saw you in another light.
In times of desperation, you were my hope.
Like an angel that has spread its wings.
And healed wounds where life did sting.

Every day I appreciate you and I'm ready to tell you so,
That maybe, if we took the next step, our love would surely
grow.
But if you want, for us just to remain friends,
Then that's just fine,
But if you're ready for the crossover, I think it's time.

Valentine

Sometimes in the year,
I wonder how much I love you so,
At other times in the year,
I realise, I don't want to let you go,
And as the years go by, my feelings do grow,
though I don't always get love right, I do try and let it show.

So, as I learn to appreciate all that you do,
And have become accustom to your habits too.
Taking you for all your worth,
To me, the salt of the earth.

So today I'd like to take this chance to say,
"I love you more and more each day."
For you to look into my heart and take the time to see,
exactly how much my river runs deep.

And even though all year round, I know your mine,
I don't often get the chance to say,
"Happy Valentines"

We Must, We Must, We Must

We must, we must, we must,
Awake with the rise of the sun.
And depart from our wooden shacks,
To ensure their work is done.
How can we live a life with such law?
That we are dragged from our beds of straw.
To attend the fields to plant tobacco and rice,
Which to us, shall hold no price.

To feed cattle, pick cotton and sugar cane,
Only to be bought into sorrow and shame.
We shall carry our babies upon our back as we work in the
deadly heat.
No time at all to relax, not even in discreet.

We must, we must, we must,
Ensure they wine and dine,
Cooking foods of pure divine from our hands and our hearts,
We shall provide this dish, with oh such flavour,
A taste that we shall be unable to savour.
Whilst they walk in our silks, such beauty flows,
Yet we are left to wear cloth for clothes.
How can we over power them, how can we sustain our pride,

How can we hold onto the passion we have inside?

We must, we must, we must
Sing our songs of love and release the voice of sorrow,
To provide a voice for the people of tomorrow.
We shall sing for our loved ones from which we are apart,
As the unison of our voices shall provide a new start.

For whippings may have bought us to our knees,
But our strength brings us back to stance,
And the weight of their shackles shall not diminish our
rhythm and dance.
We shall overcome temptation and not be taken in by such
greed,
Like those who sit on the fruits of our labour and feed.
We shall use our skills and the freedom of free will.
And in the future, they will see that we can overcome our
problems if we stand in unity,
To provide peace, tolerance and equality.

For were sure our ancestors will see,
That we haven't taken lashings for free.
No, we shall let our wounds heal.
For we never knew we could endure so much pain,
And now we know we always had the strength to reign.
For the days we all have freedom of speech so we can stand
up and speak.
Our Children, Great grandchildren and their children too,
They shall stand up as a nation and not a mere few.
They shall know each year of progression and continue to
progress,

With the strength and determination to showcase our best.
For we may go through various troubles but action will not
be in vain,
And unlike the actions of a master our solutions will not be
inhumane.
They will stand with strength and courage for one day we
will be ancestors too,
And our Children, great grandchildren and their children will
see how we came through.

Why Do I Think of You?

I wonder why I think of you, all of the time.
I wonder why you are always on my mind.

First thing in the morning and last thing at night,
Even when you're by my side and holding me tight.
Everything I do you seem to be involved,
Cause with you any problem can be solved.

I think it's because for me you are always there.
And when I feel down and out for me you always care.
I think of you even when I do standard daily things,
like listening to music, cleaning my house or whenever my
phone rings.
I wonder if you do, think of me the same,
Like when you're chilling out and playing computer games.

Do you wonder what I'm up to and if I might be free?
So, you can come on over and maybe handle me.
Or if you want, we can sit back on my sofa and chill,
whilst your content with me in your arms, as you hold me
still.

I think, I think of you,

Because I love you so.

But do you think of me, or don't you really know?

Woman

Grey dress, white apron and bowl,
Taking care to stir this pot and stitch a button hole,
Set to ironing and handwash some clothes,
Top up the coal on the stove.
Water to boil and dinner to be ready by sunset.
Sweet, sweet marionette,
She gazes into a daydream, longing to be a star,
But shall that day come, not by far.
But the day, a woman has the right to say,
The day they take a stance,
It shall be in extreme circumstance.

So back in the day, the suffer jets,
Chained themselves down,
And their strength turned it all around.

WOW, did she get the right to vote,
And now she's lost control,
Or did she find a voice to free her soul.

Pulling away from the shekels of the kitchen sink,
Been given the right to share as she thinks.
In a man's world of discipline,

She speaks up and possesses equality.
The right to stand side by side
In riches and poverty.
And as time goes by, this strength has increased,
Women hold a power that needed to be released.
Such beauty, such spirit, such soul.
So, as they took the hands of their men,
Showed them what they were worth,
To their children,
The mothers of the earth.
Daughters to follow in footsteps,
And sisters, doing it for themselves.
A wife to keep a household,
Women, no longer sitting on the shelf.

In this day and age, she can be all she wants to be,
The kind of woman with sex appeal and chemistry.
High powered jobs and status.
In her abilities we trust,
To multi-task and to come out on top.
Are the roles reversed or did they just swap?
Well, I don't know but these strong women can't be stopped.
Now it's a phenomenon, from one by one,
To stand in unison.
All my girls, all my ladies, all my sisters for true.
Take it which ever way you want,
Which ever way it's construed,
But we have the power to rule.
So, where a queen wears her crown,
Her king stands by her side,
And adorns him with honours and pride.

For we have the chance to make the difference,
And these changes we shall embrace,
As we continue to run the human race.